I0015170

Visualization

A Formal Guide To Enhance Personal Growth:
Overcoming Procrastination, Utilizing Vibration
Frequency And Law Of Attraction To Enhance Memory

*(Comprehensive Overview Of Data Visualization Using
Python)*

Johnnie Conley

TABLE OF CONTENT

Basics Of Visualization

We are all acquainted with individuals who appear to possess everything. This individual does not exhibit the highest level of intelligence, perseverance, or physical attractiveness that we have encountered. Nevertheless, this individual possesses the ability to consistently draw in favorable individuals and situations, enabling them to manifest their wants and desires effectively. It looks effortless. He possesses a particular expertise that he fosters and subsequently engenders an affinity for all the circumstances, situations, and individuals that will facilitate the utilization of his abilities in pursuit of his aspirations.

Therefore, you frequently ponder the reason behind the apparent ease with which prosperous individuals effortlessly draw things and circumstances towards themselves. Frequently, they encounter superior employment and business prospects, exceptional interpersonal connections, and contented personal lives. In actuality, these individuals of accomplishment have attained mastery in the skill of manifesting and attracting outcomes, a practice that has been long embraced by scholars, accomplished figures in various fields, and spiritual mystics across the ages.

Indeed, the human mind possesses the inherent ability to generate and actualize any desired outcomes in life, be it the attainment of our envisioned professional vocation, the discovery of an ideal companion, the acquisition of coveted possessions, or the cultivation of desired interpersonal connections. The depths of our subconscious generate vibrations that are subsequently emitted into the vast expanse of the universe through the medium of our thoughts. These oscillations will harmonize with fellow oscillations operating at identical frequencies to yield the desired outcome as per your subconscious inclination.

The cognitive processes and latent mental constructs residing within our subconscious hold the capacity to exert a profound influence over the eventual outcome of various situations and circumstances. It is imperative that we exert authority over our subconscious mind and assert control over its actions. An effective approach is to employ the technique of mentally picturing the outcome we aspire to achieve.

What is visualization?

Visualization is essentially the act of reconstructing all the sensory perceptions, auditory stimuli, and visual representations of one's intended scenario or condition within the realms of the mind. Consequently, visualization is an exceptional method that harnesses the potency of one's thoughts to materialize and bring forth our desired outcomes in life. It rests upon the fundamental notion that any concept that we can conceive and envision with great clarity within our cognitive faculties materializes within our tangible existence.

The Historical Evolution of Visual Representation

The act of visualization has been long engaged in by devoted monks and enlightened mystics throughout the Eastern region for an extensive period of time. Nevertheless, this method gained popularity in Western societies following the publication of "The Science of Getting Rich" by Wallace Wattles, an esteemed American proponent of visualization. Consequently, athletes, statesmen, and accomplished entrepreneurs have diligently embraced this remarkable practice.

The Underpinnings of Visualization from a Scientific Perspective

Visualization is a remarkable manifestation technique that is employed by numerous individuals who have achieved great success across a wide range of industries including economics, business, entertainment, athletics, engineering, and scientific endeavors. Indeed, visualization is grounded in scientific principles. It is widely acknowledged among researchers that individuals engage a common neural region when they mentally envision an action or scenario, compared to when they physically execute the action or find themselves present in a given situation. Numerous studies affirm that individuals who have experienced a stroke can effectively engage their cognitive functions to facilitate muscular movement through the process of mental imagery alone. Specifically, through visualizing the action of specific body parts, such as fingers or toes, these patients can stimulate their brain to generate corresponding physical responses. Numerous healthcare professionals maintain the belief that engaging in mental imagery of moving a specific muscle or limb, even in the presence of paralysis resulting from a stroke, enhances cerebral blood flow sufficiently to mitigate the magnitude and scope of tissue necrosis. This serves as evidence of the formidable ability of visualization to bring about desired outcomes. This serves as evidence that the practice of visualization possesses the ability to manifest our aspirations into actuality.

Visualization and Athletic Performance

Athletes have been aware of this power for several decades. Indeed, the instruction provided has encompassed the incorporation of creative visualization exercises. Esteemed athletes like Tiger Woods have employed the faculty of imagination to attain their target score. Prominent athletes in the field of running prioritize the regular use of mental imagery, wherein they frequently envision themselves partaking in races and accomplishing their desired time goals. They imagine in detail. They engage in the act of envisaging and constructing each individual step, as well as the entire distance they cover, within the realm of their thoughts. Consequently, these athletes successfully achieved their desired timing during the race.

To substantiate this claim, an investigation was undertaken which entailed the participation of a group of individuals skilled in the sport of basketball. Fifty percent of the team was assigned to engage in physical training, whereas the remaining fifty percent was tasked with engaging in mental training exclusively. The results were outstanding. Individuals who engaged in the practice of employing visualization and imagination techniques to train exhibited equivalent levels of proficiency as their counterparts who underwent conventional physical training.

Famous Personalities Who Employed Creative Visualization

Numerous other prominent figures exercised this ability to materialize their desired outcomes in life. The prominent artist Beyonce has utilized this method prior to every stage appearance. She diligently honed her mental prowess to attain fame and master the art of delivering impeccable performances before vast audiences. Jay-Z, her spouse, likewise employed this strategy to successfully finalize record deals worth millions. Renowned athletes like Kobe Bryant, Lebron James, and Michael Phelps have employed the utilization of visualization and imagination to attain unparalleled athletic prowess. Oprah Winfrey, renowned as the Queen of Talk, has effectively employed this strategy to achieve unprecedented levels of influence and wealth, propelling her to become one of the most influential and affluent women in the contemporary global landscape. Numerous prominent celebrities and successful businesspeople employ this methodology, including individuals such as Arnold Schwarzenegger, Bill Gates, and Jim Carrey.

Mere thoughts are powerful. However, it can be argued that images possess a greater level of impact. When one directs their attention towards their aspirations and visualizes the realization of their desired life in their mind, thereby embedding it into their subconscious, they are embarking upon the path to its attainment. The cosmic order realigns itself to manifest propitious circumstances, individuals, and scenarios capable of facilitating the actualization of your aspirations.

The Precise Mechanism Behind The Visualization Process

Mechanism of Operation

The human mind consists of two distinct constituents, namely the conscious mind and the subconscious mind. We contend that our conscious reasoning, as well as any notions we consistently entertain, seep into our subconscious or imaginative faculties. The subconscious mind bears semblance to a computational system. It lacks independent discernment to distinguish between excellence and inferiority, between truth and falsehood. It sufficiently addresses the stated value, regardless of its existence.

When the conscious mind repeatedly presents the same idea to the subconscious, it begins to give credence to the idea and sets in motion the process of manifesting it.

The multitude of experiences we have amassed in our lives is stored within our subconscious, having achieved entrance therein. It also possesses the capacity to tap into the collective consciousness, where no concept is inconceivable.

The subsequent actions of the subconscious often give rise to complications wherein our recurring thoughts manifest.

I recently came across a narrative that exemplifies the intricacies of visualization in a captivating yet perilous manner. Therefore, exercise caution regarding what you inquire about. You could get it.').

A gentleman had a progeny who suffered from a severe case of arthritic inflammation in the joints. He made numerous attempts to experiment with various drugs, but the outcomes were unsuccessful. Whenever he would encounter someone, he would consistently express, in a figurative manner, his unwavering commitment to ensuring the well-being of his daughter by stating, "I would sacrifice my utmost effort to care for my child."

Strangely enough, a few years later, while he was traveling in a vehicle, he encountered an incident that resulted in the tragic dismemberment of his right arm. Within a few days, the inflammation in his child's joints was effectively treated!

In order to fully grasp the functioning of visualization, it is imperative that we comprehend the fact that images serve as the transcendent form of communication within the subconscious mind.

While it demonstrates comparable proficiency in word conversion, its efficiency is further amplified when working with visual representations. Hence, the efficacy of visualization lies in its ability to prompt the subconscious mind to manifest desired outcomes. It is equally essential to envision solely the final result, rather than fixating on the procedure. We must conscientiously communicate our desires to the subconscious. It is the responsibility of the subconscious mind to determine the approach for its resolution.

A single photograph carries the weight of a thousand words. We have indeed encountered that statement before! This assertion has never been more valid than when it pertains to the utilization of visualization. Visualization is an exceptional tool for managing ailments and health concerns in your life. Visualization, a contemplative method, employs photographs or imagery to stabilize the mind and enhance our faculties.

The objective is to restore the body to a state of complete wellbeing. The human mind is divided into two distinct sides, namely the rational left hemisphere and the creative right hemisphere. A substantial portion of our existence is devoted to utilizing the cerebral hemisphere associated with logic and reason, commonly referred to as the left side of the brain. By employing the technique of visualization, we acknowledge and nurture our inherent capacity for innovative thinking, while simultaneously achieving a state of mental equilibrium. This equilibrium facilitates the innate healing processes of the body and mind.

Visualization utilizes visual imagery to alter one's emotional state, consequently modulating one's sensory perceptions, resulting in a tangible sensation that has the potential to alleviate or eradicate symptoms.

The mental disposition is characterized by emotional experience, just as emotional experience gives rise to sensations. The individual's physiological constitution is acquired through lived encounters. When a sensation is experienced, it elicits a physical response. Visualization products offer compelling imagery that stimulate the mind, eliciting emotive responses that give rise to a profound sensory experience.

That is the precise means by which you establish a connection between your mind and body.

Often, we tend to adopt a rational, logical mindset in order to ensure our survival. This disparity fosters inequity within the realm of cognition. By yielding to our conceptualized intellect, we tap into the inherent connection between the mind and body, facilitating the restoration of mental equilibrium and fostering an openness to transformation and rejuvenation.

Research has demonstrated that negative emotions have a detrimental impact on both our physical immune system and our mental well-being.

Experiencing negative emotions hinders and impedes our progress towards our goals and authentic selves.

impedes the mind from achieving our desired goals. Positive emotions have a significant impact on strengthening the body's immune system and fostering a harmonized mental state, thereby facilitating personal growth.

The visualization process is straightforward.

1) Find a serene location.

2) Specify your intent.

3) Direct your attention to the breath and engage in intentional respiration.

4) Beginning your visualization.

Successful implementation of visualization generally entails a two-week timeframe and is best practiced in both the morning and the evening, prior to bedtime. Nevertheless, a substantial number of individuals observe results following their initial attempt. In order to achieve a positive outcome, it is imperative to clearly articulate your intention while also sincerely embracing and believing in its potential success.

When Don't Affirmations Work?

An affirmation represents a declaration, a verity that you assert to exert an influence on your life. Positive assertions have the capacity to alter one's perception and manifest a favorable transformation in their tangible reality.

Nevertheless, simply reiterating a phrase or affirmation without dedicating effort to the words amounts to nothing more than wishful thinking.

Please consider your affirmation as the equivalent of a jet airplane. Visualize with me an exquisite, glistening aircraft gracefully positioned on the runway. You hold the position of the captain, yet unless you activate the engines, the jet will remain stationary on the runway. By manually advancing the throttle, the engines spring to action, propelling the aircraft forward before gracefully ascending into the serene azure heavens. The essence driving your affirmations will bestow upon them the power to soar.

The initial stage entails having faith in the veracity of your assertions. Infuse vitality into them. Experience the surge of their energy permeating within you. The fusion of conviction with the force of your emotional intensity indeed acts as the propelling force behind your flight.

As previously mentioned, in situations where emotions and intellect are at odds, the prevailing victor will invariably be the realm of emotions. As aforementioned, the Universe unfailingly heeds the more emphatic summons.

The thoughts and preoccupations that occupy your mind will inevitably materialize in the tangible realm. The cosmos perpetually perceives both your spoken words and emotional expressions.

In bygone years, I would allocate the initial half-hour of each morning to engage in prayer and meditation, with the intention of cultivating my financial prosperity on a spiritual level. I sincerely ignited the profound spiritual essence within me through my devout observance and contemplation, thereby experiencing a deep union with my inherent benevolence. If only I could have prolonged those invaluable instances of unity with my financial aspirations.

Indeed, following my morning meditations, it was customary for me to promptly assess my financial standing, which consequently resulted in a significant portion of my subsequent twenty-three hours being consumed by a distressing preoccupation with money and the perceived insufficiency thereof.

I set the Universal Laws of Attraction and Correspondence into play, which returned to me as an unending cycle of financial challenges.

Any action we undertake will be reciprocated with amplified consequences.

As my religious beliefs became stronger, I broke free from that demoralizing pattern by redirecting my focus and wholeheartedly embracing an attitude of abundance throughout each passing day. As I diligently focused my attention and intellectual faculties on the pursuit of abundance, the boundless forces of the Universe graciously unhinged the barriers of fiscal growth, while I embraced a mindset steeped in prosperity.

On what are you directing your attention during the course of the day?

I had the pleasure of attending a Christian Science Lecture where I came across a particularly captivating story that stands out among my favorites. Regrettably, the identity of the speaker has been consigned to the annals of history, yet the imagery they evoked continues to reverberate within me even now.

He recounted a narrative of an elderly woman who possessed scarce sustenance. Her offspring had abandoned her, her spouse had departed to pursue a relationship with another individual, and her dwelling was deteriorating. Filled with sorrow about her existence, she sought solace from her clergyman.

The minister inquired gently, "What supplications have you presented to the Divine?

In a solemn manner, tears welling up in her eyes, she whispered softly, "Throughout my life, all I have beseeched of the divine has been a meager sustenance and a shelter to call home."

The moral message conveyed by this narrative may appear severe; nevertheless, the underlying lesson is unequivocal - every individual ultimately receives precisely what they request. Hence, exercise caution in your entreaties to the divine realm.

A hundred years ago, there existed a tale about an Irish youngster who carefully allocated a small quantity of bread and cheese for his arduous journey across the Atlantic towards the United States. He vigilantly monitored his provisions; however, the bread succumbed to mold and the cheese underwent spoilage as time progressed. During the entirety of the expedition, he attentively absorbed the cheerful anecdotes exchanged by his fellow passengers during their nourishing repasts. It was only when they approached the coastline that he became aware that his ticket encompassed the provision of daily meals. Your entry to this existence encompasses ample opportunities.

In the King James Version of the Bible, John 10:10 contains Jesus' proclamation where He declares, 'My purpose for arriving is to grant them the gift of existence, characterized by greater abundance.'

Frequently, we restrict ourselves by entertaining erroneous and self-imposed beliefs. How often do we refrain from seeking trivialities when the Universe stands ready to bestow upon us exponentially greater gifts, if only we would graciously embrace them? It is apparent that you were destined for great success. You were born success-filled. It's your nature.

If you are encountering difficulties in attaining prosperity, commence by enumerating your fortunate circumstances. Express gratitude to the divine for your blessings each morning and evening. Conduct a thorough inspection of your residence, imparting a ceremonial touch and divine benediction upon each piece of furniture, garment, dining utensil, and the refrigerator housing your sustenance. Compile a comprehensive inventory of your blessings, and observe how this catalog expands both your perspective of appreciation and your monetary resources.

Overcome fear and uncertainty by firmly believing in the truth of your affirmations and expressions. Infuse those positive statements with the self-assurance arising from your emotional state.

As part of my approach to working with clients, it is common for me to provide affirmations, akin to medical professionals prescribing medications to their patients. Rather than taking two pills daily, I would recommend that they engage in the practice of reciting an affirmation every hour, consistently throughout the day.

Devote a portion of each day to cultivating optimistic reflections regarding wealth, plenty, well-being, and affection.

An additional factor contributing to the lack of attainment of your desired outcome pertains to the process of outlining.

Exercises And Methods For Enhancing Visualization Abilities

There exist two significant visualization exercises:
• Impede focus
• Conceptualizing the relationship between the mind and body • Cognitive imagery incorporating both mind and body • Mental representation integrating mind-body connection • Visualizing the unity of the mind and body

Both serve as an invaluable instrument for augmenting imagination and concentration. One can engage in communication with their subconscious mind by employing the faculty of imagination. The cognitive faculties have the capacity to focus on manifold responsibilities, thereby potentially giving rise to a sense of urgency, unease, and strain. It may arise from a lack of concentration and errors. It is imperative that you enhance your concentration by directing your attention towards the present moment. The focal point is typically readjusted to sustain your attention on the current occurrence rather than diverting your thoughts towards prior or future occurrences. This practice will assist you in managing your emotions and enhancing your ability to focus on the present circumstances. It can be implemented as a therapeutic practice and a form of visual exercise. Engaging in the training program will refine your perspective, allowing you to perceive and interpret various phenomena more effectively.

Visualization Exercises

There exist two crucial visualization exercises that can be employed as means to enhance concentration.

Blocked Concentration

This task can be executed through two different approaches, wherein the initial approach involves utilization of the black dot. Simply create a circular marking of a diameter equivalent to that of a quarter using black ink on a sheet of paper, and subsequently affix said paper onto the vertical surface. It should be situated at a level that corresponds to your eye level when in a seated position. Please take a seat in the chair and allow yourself to unwind both mentally and physically. Maintain your attention fixed on the dot, and gaze unwaveringly at it without any eye movement.

The focal point of your attention should be solely directed towards the black dot, refraining from any additional distraction or wandering thoughts. In the event of any presence of distracting thoughts, it is advised to sustain your focus solely on the black dot. Commence this exercise regimen by engaging in a five-minute routine consistently, and sustain this practice for a duration of 90 days. It has the potential to facilitate profound advancements in focus and imaginative capabilities.

Second Method

An alternative approach to practice the exercise is to employ a candle. Ignite the candle with the purpose of fixating one's attention upon the flickering flame, akin to the act of concentrating on the black dot. Direct your attention solely to the flame of the candle, as this will yield favorable outcomes. In the event that you encounter any mental distractions, direct your attention towards the fire as a means to regain focus.

The technique is relatively straightforward to utilize, enabling individuals to effectively govern their mental faculties, thereby amplifying its efficacy. If one desires to facilitate the achievement of their goals, they may regulate their desires in order to enhance their imaginative capacity.

Cognitive and Physical Imagery

This activity serves as a secondary exercise aimed at enhancing your imaginative capabilities. Please kindly close your eyes and visualize a serene image, perhaps that of a vast ocean with undulating waves. Envision the scene with utmost lucidity, taking note of the vibrant hues of sand, water, and various other components. Envision yourself strolling across the sandy terrain, feeling the grainy particles between your toes, as you gradually extend your hand forward. Envision your hand and fingers vividly within the confines of your imagination.

• Progress onward and observe your environs in a deliberate manner, taking note of the azure water, sandy shores, and verdant foliage. Develop an authentic experience in order to attain your intended goals. It will provide you with opportunities to experience various physical advantages in your life.

• By engaging in visualization exercises, individuals are able to attain the advantages of enhanced focus and concentration, requiring the mental projection and contemplation of desired images. One can facilitate their practice by utilizing vibrant imaginations.

If you desire to fully reap the rewards of these exercises, it is recommended to engage in consistent, ongoing practice. It will enable you to enhance your concentration, leading to numerous emotional and psychological advantages.

4-Exploring the Libraries

"Within the pages of this literary work, we shall delve into the realm of data visualization in the Python programming language, utilizing a trio of esteemed libraries, namely:

Matplotlib

Pandas

Seaborn

Matplotlib

This is a Python library utilized for generating 2D graphs and plots through the utilization of Python scripts. One may find a module called pyplot within the package, which offers convenient functionality for creating plots. This module includes features that facilitate the control of font properties, line styles, formatting of axes, and more. It is capable of generating various types of plots, including histograms, power spectra, bar charts, error charts, and more. It is employed in conjunction with the NumPy library. Consequently, it is employed on the NumPy arrays.

The library was established in 2002 under the guidance of John Hunter. The installation of matplotlib can be carried out by utilizing the pip package manager that is bundled with Python. If Python has been successfully installed on your computer, then it is highly likely that pip has also been automatically installed. In the Python 3.X environment, the package manager is accessed by utilizing the pip3 command. The installation can be executed by inputting the following command in the terminal of the operating system: "

pip3 install matplotlib

In order to confirm the successful installation, please attempt to import the pyplot module from the library by executing the following command within the Python terminal:

Import the pyplot module from matplotlib as plt.

If the installation has been completed successfully, you will be returned to the Python terminal interface, as illustrated below:

In the event that this condition is not met, a failure will be triggered.

Pandas

This Python package is freely available with an open source license and encompasses a plethora of tools specifically designed for the analysis of data. Pandas offers a wide array of data structures that enable users to store and manipulate their data effectively. The library offers a wide range of callable methods specifically designed for conducting data analysis tasks.

It should be noted that the Pandas library was developed based on the Matplotlib framework. This elucidates the reason for its inclusion of data visualization capabilities. Pandas provides the capability to generate various kinds of visual representations using the data contained in a dataframe. One advantage of using Pandas is its capability to efficiently load data from diverse file formats.

The installation of the Pandas library can be accomplished by utilizing the pip package manager. This package manager is included with Python, as previously mentioned. To successfully add the Pandas library to your system, execute the provided command in the terminal of your operating system:

pip3 install pandas

I have employed the pip3 command as I am utilizing Python 3.X on my system.
In order to ascertain the success of the installation, kindly attempt to import the Pandas library by executing the

subsequent command in the Python terminal:

pandas is imported as pd

If the installation has been completed successfully, the Python terminal will be returned to you in the following manner:

In the event that the installation was unsuccessful, an error message will be produced.

Seaborn

This particular library serves the purpose of data visualization and is built upon the foundation of the Matplotlib library. With the utilization of Seaborn, visually appealing charts can be generated. The library excels in enabling various data visualization requirements, such as the mapping of color to a variable or the utilization of faceting.

41

The Seaborn library effectively interacts with data that is stored within a Pandas data frame.

The tool grants a substantial degree of adaptability to its users during the process of plot creation, as it offers an extensive array of plotting styles from which the user can select. The library demonstrates proficient efficacy in associating the features to your data.

The Seaborn library can be installed by utilizing the pip package manager. Kindly execute the subsequent command on the terminal interface of your operating system: "

pip3 install seaborn

"To ascertain the success of the installation, it is necessary to import the library by executing the following command on the Python terminal:

Employ the seaborn module for data visualization.

"If the installation was successful, the Python terminal should appear as depicted in the illustration below:

In the event that the installation proves unsuccessful, an error will be generated.

Folium

The folium library is utilized in Python to visualize geographic data. By utilizing this library, individuals have the capability to generate maps for any location, given that the longitude and latitude coordinates of the specific area are readily available. Additionally, the folium library possesses the capability to generate interactive maps, enabling the user to manipulate the zoom level of the map post rendering. This feature proves to be highly practical and beneficial.

43

By utilizing the folium library, it is possible to generate diverse forms of leaflet maps. Because of the interactive attributes present in the maps produced by the folium library, the library has proven to be advantageous in the construction of dashboards.

Prior to utilizing the folium library, it is necessary to install it. This task can be accomplished by utilizing the pip package manager. To execute the given action, simply input the following command within the terminal of your operating system:

```
pip3 install folium
```

The installation process is expected to conclude within a matter of seconds to minutes.

CRM, or Customer Relationship Management

The primary aim of customer relationship management (CRM) is to acquire and retain customers, thereby enabling businesses to formulate strategies centered around customer needs and augment customer allegiance. In order to enhance your rapport with customers, it is imperative to gather pertinent information and conduct precise analysis. By employing appropriate data mining technologies, the data gathered can be utilized for the purpose of scrutinizing and ascertaining strategies for enhancing customer relationships.

Fraud Detection
Have you ever lent someone money, only for them to abruptly cut off all communication afterwards? That serves as an illustration of fraudulent activity, albeit limited in scope. Each year, financial institutions such as banks

suffer a loss of nearly one billion dollars due to deceitful customers. Conventional methods employed for fraud detection are intricate and require a considerable amount of time. Data mining employs various statistical and mathematical algorithms to discern concealed and significant patterns within datasets. It is imperative to employ a fraud detection system with the aim of safeguarding the entirety of the information encompassed within the dataset, while concurrently ensuring the protection of individual user's data. Supervised data mining models possess a dataset comprised of training or sample records, enabling the system to effectively identify and classify specific customers as fraudulent. It is possible to create a model utilizing this information. The goal of this model is to ascertain the presence or absence of fraudulent claimants and accompanying documents.

Lie Detection

Apprehending criminals poses no significant challenge, yet extracting the truth from them poses an exorbitant level of difficulty. This task presents considerable difficulty. Numerous police departments and law enforcement agencies presently employ data mining methodologies to surveil all forms of communication involving suspected individuals involved in terrorism, probe prior criminal activities, and so forth. In addition, text mining is incorporated into the data mining algorithms employed for this purpose. During this procedure, the algorithm systematically examines multiple text files and datasets to ascertain concealed patterns within the dataset. The information utilized within this format frequently lacks organization and coherence. These algorithms perform a comparative analysis between the present output and past outputs in order to construct a model for lie detection.

Financial Banking

Financial institutions have undergone a transformation and are now in the process of digitalizing all customer transactions and data. By employing data mining algorithms and techniques, bankers are able to address a multitude of business-related concerns and challenges. These models can be utilized to discern diverse trends, correlations, and patterns in the collected data. Bankers have the capacity to employ these methodologies in managing substantial amounts of data. It is more convenient for managers and experts to utilize these data and correlations in order to enhance their ability to obtain, focus on, differentiate, sustain, and uphold diverse customer profiles.

Challenges

Data mining is a critical undertaking of significant magnitude and tremendous efficacy. However, there are numerous challenges that may arise during the implementation or execution of these algorithms. The difficulties encountered pertain to data, performance, methodologies, and approaches employed in the field of data mining. The efficacy of the data mining process can only be realized when one duly identifies and effectively resolves the encountered problems or challenges.

Noisy and Incomplete Data

As previously discussed, the process of extracting valuable insights and patterns from vast quantities of data is commonly referred to as data mining. One must bear in mind the fact that real-time data collection is characterized by its incompleteness, noise, and heterogeneity. It proves challenging to ascertain the reliability and accuracy of the collected data. These issues arise due to human errors or imprecise measuring instruments. Suppose you are the manager of a retail chain. Your responsibility entails obtaining the contact information of each customer who surpasses the expenditure threshold of $1000 at your establishment. Once a customer of this nature is identified, it is required to transmit a notification to the designated accounting personnel, who will subsequently proceed to input the relevant information. The individual responsible for accounting may input an inaccurate figure into the dataset, resulting in erroneous data. Additionally, there is a possibility that certain customers may hastily input an incorrect number or commit such an error due to various reasons. Additional clients may have reservations about sharing their number due to concerns regarding privacy. These circumstances present difficulties to the data mining process.

Data Distribution

Real-world data is stored on various platforms within a distributed computing environment spanning multiple platforms. The data can be stored on the World Wide Web, individual computing platforms, or within a structured repository. This presents a challenge in terms of transferring the data from these sources to a central data repository, as there are varying technical and organizational considerations that need to be taken into account. For example, certain regional offices may opt to store their data on their respective servers for the purpose of data storage. It is not feasible to consolidate the data from various regional offices onto a single server upon careful consideration. Hence, if one desires to engage in data mining, it is imperative to construct the requisite algorithms and implement tools that facilitate the efficient extraction of substantial datasets.

Complex Data

Business enterprises presently gather data from various sources, and this data exhibits heterogeneity. It is capable of incorporating diverse forms of multimedia content, encompassing videos, audios, images, as well as intricate data types like time series and spatial data, among others. It poses a challenge for individuals to effectively handle and analyze this data or derive valuable insights from it. In order to obtain the necessary information, it is often crucial to fine-tune novel tools, methodologies, and technologies.

Performance

The effectiveness of a data visualization model is directly dependent on the algorithm employed and the level of efficiency it possesses. The performance of the model is contingent upon the methodology employed in its development. In the event that the algorithm is inadequately crafted, it will have a substantial impact on the efficiency of the process.

Protection of Data and Safeguarding Privacy

Data mining poses a significant concern in terms of data governance, privacy, and security. Suppose you are a merchant who evaluates a customer's buying behavior. In order to accomplish this, it is necessary to gather comprehensive data pertaining to your customers, including their purchasing patterns, preferences, and other relevant particulars. It is necessary for you to gather this information, and obtaining explicit consent from your customers may not be obligatory in this regard.

Data Visualization

Data visualization plays a crucial role in the examination of data during the process of data mining. This is the sole method by which you, or an enterprise, can visualize the distinct patterns and trends within the dataset. Businesses and data scientists should endeavor to ascertain the intended message conveyed by the data and the variables within the dataset. It is equally significant to grasp the intended message conveyed by the data. There are instances in which it proves challenging to present the data in a manner that is readily comprehensible. Certain input data points, or variables, may yield intricate outputs. Hence, it is imperative to discern and implement effective and precise methodologies pertaining to data visualization in order to achieve success.

Improving Cognitive Concentration Via The Practice Of Meditation

In the subsequent chapter, we shall delve into three fundamental meditation methodologies you may employ. There exist numerous variations of these meditation methodologies, yet it is necessary for you to experience each one in order to ascertain which one yields the most favorable results for you. It is imperative to bear in mind the underlying purpose for engaging in meditation. You're not solely engaging in this for the substantial generation of inner tranquility and serenity it entails.

As alluded to earlier in a preceding section, the efficacy of meditation in mitigating hypertension, fostering profound mental tranquility, and alleviating significant levels of stress has been substantiated by numerous empirical investigations. Meditation has its effectiveness, although it may not produce the anticipated benefits.

You are seeking a highly specific advantage derived from meditation, namely an exceptional level of concentration akin to a laser-like focus. This is the key. This is the determining factor behind your decision to embrace a meditation practice. It is imperative to possess such focus in order to transform your personal visions of an alternative reality into a tangible existence that you inhabit. Please bear the following points in your thoughts.

The essence of meditation

Despite the diverse array of meditation practices stemming from various philosophical and spiritual traditions across the globe, an underlying similarity unifies them all. Each of these diverse practices encompasses distinct terminologies, methodologies, and systems; nonetheless, at their core, they share a fundamental similarity.

A unifying aspect between them is their ability to cultivate a heightened awareness of the present moment within individuals. You do not ruminate on historical events. You do not engage in the handling of past recollections. You do not have concerns about the future. One refrains from making conjectures or suppositions regarding future outcomes. Instead, you merely direct your attention to your present moment, meticulously observing each passing second. You attain a profound state of tranquility as your capacity for concentration becomes honed to a laser-like precision, singularly directed towards a specific point in both time and space. You are perpetually situated in the realm of timeless existence.

Consider your mind as a vast expanse of water. At the uppermost level, a considerable amount of dramatic events are anticipated. There will be a considerable amount of stress, concerns, anxieties, and frustrations. However, should you descend to a depth of 200 feet, you would encounter a remarkably tranquil environment. Occasionally, minor turbulence persists; nonetheless, the prevailing atmosphere remains tranquil as it remains detached from the tumultuous events transpiring on the surface.

Now, should one decide to submerge oneself entirely, and by this I mean reaching a point merely a foot above the seabed, they would encounter a state of complete tranquility. That is a manifestation of the way your mind functions. There exists a serene core within oneself that facilitates the release of an immense level of concentration.

Nonetheless, achieving such a state can only be attained through the disciplined cultivation of one's mindset, whereby the individual transcends the distractions and disturbances emanating from the superficial aspects of their existence, delving deep into the realms of inner tranquility until they reach the very essence at the core of their being.

There exist three methodologies/procedures/approaches at your disposal to accomplish this task. Furthermore, as previously stated, it should be noted that although various iterations exist, the multitude of meditation techniques ultimately converge into these three fundamental approaches.

Counting your breath

Engaging in the act of mindful respiration serves as a straightforward method of cultivating a meditative state.

You have the option to locate a tranquil space where you may assume a relaxed position. There is no requirement for you to assume the lotus position. There is no obligation for you to assume the meditative posture popularly associated with the Buddha. Kindly assume your usual seating position to ensure your comfort. Nonetheless, it is imperative not to be excessively at ease to the point of dozing off.

Maintaining proper posture, specifically by ensuring a straight back, is of utmost importance in order to maintain optimal focus and concentration. The commencement of this activity entails the act of closing one's eyes and engaging in deliberate, measured breaths. You iterate this process multiple times and subsequently decrease the pace of your respiration, while directing your conscious focus towards the inhalation and exhalation occurring within your physical being. It is imperative that you utilize your diaphragm for breathing. This pertains to your abdominal area, commonly referred to as the lower portion of your stomach region. It is recommended that you consider forming a cup shape with your hands or interlocking them beneath your belly button, subsequently directing your breath into this space you have created. Please execute this task at a slower pace while maintaining attention on your breath.

After engaging in this practice for a prolonged duration, a sense of tranquility ensues, with one's attention intently fixed solely on the act of breathing. You stop worrying. Thoughts are no longer manifest to the degree to which you pass judgment upon them or allow them to induce anxiety. They effortlessly meander through the corridors of your thoughts, akin to ethereal cloud formations. The act of focusing solely on your breath is the singular sensory emphasis employed in the practice of counting your breath. This task necessitates being spread out across multiple days and weeks.

Once more, the gauge of achievement lies in the extent of concentration one can maintain on their breath, undeterred by distractions. This practice proves to be remarkable as, over time, one ceases to pass judgment on their thoughts. They assume the resemblance of transitory clouds, devoid of significance or relevance. The crucial factor lies in the awareness of your breathing pattern being the sole focus of your attention.

Transcendental meditation

There are notable similarities between transcendental meditation and the act of counting one's breath. You undergo an identical procedure akin to the act of enumerating your breaths. The significant contrast lies in the practice of silent mantra recitation associated with transcendental meditation. One does not articulate their mantra verbally. One does not verbalize it. One refrains from uttering even a whisper—such is the silence. You say it mentally.

How does this work? You shall vocalize the mantra subsequent to inhaling and subsequent to exhaling. This technique possesses considerable efficacy as, through repetitive reinforcement over multiple occurrences spanning several days, your mantra assumes a pivotal role in shaping your pattern of respiration. Gradually, your attention shifts from your breath to your chosen mantra. Your mantra serves as the focal point around which your attention gravitates.

Now, it is of utmost importance to bear in mind that your chosen mantra word ought to possess a single syllable or vowel, and it should hold no intrinsic meaning. This is really important. It is unacceptable for the word to be something resembling 'mom' or 'dad'. When a word is employed, it elicits cognitive processes. The primary objective of transcendental meditation is to eliminate or eradicate one's thoughts.

When transcendental meditation is practiced correctly, one's focus becomes so profoundly attuned to the mantra that the emergence of thoughts is effectively inhibited. You are incapable of generating ideas and subsequently evaluating them. One should refrain from becoming overly emotional due to one's judgement. This form of meditation engenders a profound state of tranquility and serenity, along with a surge of vitality.

It enjoys a widespread international following due to its straightforward and refined nature. Direct your attention solely on the mantra, and all other aspects will be attended to. Your breath seamlessly integrates into the panning practice, accompanying your concentrated recitation of your chosen mantra.

Single object focus

The practice of meditation focused solely on a single object is a distinct and disparate method. If one does not have a particular inclination or preference for entering a dimly lit chamber or a serene, isolated environment, and partaking in the act of mindfulness by regulating one's breathing, an alternative approach could be adopting a practice of concentration on a singular object. You simply require a dedicated period of uninterrupted time. This is really important. It is imperative to allocate an ample amount of time for engaging in this meditation practice. The only requirement is for you to be in a state of comfortable seating.

Once more, it is not necessary for you to succumb to sleep; rather, you only need to maintain an upright posture or position yourself in such a manner as to inhibit the onset of sleep. Afterwards, you proceed to direct your visual focus towards an object. It may serve as a literary resource in your personal library. It could potentially be a writing instrument resting upon your desk, or alternatively, a tree situated beyond the confines of your windowpane. The most crucial aspect is dedicating your entire meditation period solely to the observation of an object.

When one engages in the act of observation, they navigate the external confines or limits of the subject matter and activate their innate inquisitiveness. It is crucial to emphasize that in instances of curiosity, one is not posing inquiries. This distinction epitomizes the significant contrast between this variant of curiosity and conventional curiosity. When one is in a state of curiosity, it is customary to inquire extensively.

As an instance, let us consider the scenario where one observes a wallet resting upon the ground. Without delay, one would inquire as to the individual responsible for dropping this wallet. Could this wallet have been inadvertently dropped, misplaced by the owner, or potentially involved in a criminal act? Numerous inquiries arise. The type of curiosity I am referring to is not of that nature.

Alternatively, during single object focus meditation, one directs their attention to the perimeters of an object, exhibiting curiosity. Subsequently, the meditator observes and explores various aspects of said object, such as the play of light upon it, its hue, and proceeds to delve deeper into its intricate details. You seem uninterested in seeking the reason. You are simply seeking additional and increasingly comprehensive information. During the entirety of your meditation session, you fully engage and focus on a single object.

This meditation technique proves highly efficacious as it facilitates the purification of one's mind, enabling the individual to eliminate any prevailing thoughts. By concentrating their creative and focusing abilities solely on a specific object, practitioners train their minds to enhance attentiveness and reduce distractions. Additionally, the mind's tendency to inquire and process multiple inputs concurrently diminishes, fostering a state of tranquility. You do not attend to your respiration. One does not employ the use of a mantra. Simply direct your attention towards an object, and employing this approach results in significant mental relaxation. You achieve a state of mental relaxation when you practice single object focus.

There is no definitive correctness or incorrectness in relation to your selection among the three meditation methodologies elucidated previously. Each individual's cognitive processes vary. We possess distinct cognitive habits and patterns, frequently stemming from our diverse experiences and backgrounds. The crucial element lies in delineating the method that enhances your concentration to the greatest extent and persevering in its practice. This is how one can augment their level of concentration.

It is crucial to bear in mind that the primary objective of your meditation practice is not solely to attain inner tranquility and serenity, although these advantages can undoubtedly be acquired. The principal purpose underlying your engagement in meditation lies in augmenting and improving your capacity for sustained concentration. You will require it in order to facilitate creative visualization.

What Are Your Aspirations And Ambitions In Life?

Many individuals develop ambiguous ideas regarding their aspirations in life. If one were to attempt to elicit precise particulars from them, nevertheless, they would struggle to provide a concrete answer.

I aspire to attain substantial wealth – To what extent?

I desire a substantial automobile – What type of substantial automobile?

I aspire to become self-employed - In what specific field of work would this be?

Can you discern the emergence of a discernible pattern? Vagueness is the prevailing trend that is becoming apparent. If you provide ambiguous responses to evident inquiries in life, they will never be regarded as acceptable.

Where are you going? I don't know

At what age did you complete your schooling? – I can't remember

May I inquire about your preference for this evening's meal? – I don't know

Providing ambiguous responses to such significant inquiries holds greater significance in influencing the outcomes attained than one might anticipate. In order to successfully accomplish your objectives, it is imperative that you possess the necessary knowledge to evaluate your progress and determine the specific direction to strive for.

I desire to purchase a vehicle, and I have noticed that you possess a car.

I desire an elegant vehicle - It exudes a higher level of sophistication compared to your previous one.

I desire an elegant automobile that surpasses the sophistication of my neighbor's distinguished vehicle.

The quantification and qualification of the ideal car for this individual were articulated in the third sentence, at the very least. Therefore, in order to locate the automobile that fulfills his desires, it is imperative that it surpasses the one possessed by his affluent neighbor. If he were able to mentally conceptualize a specific make and model of automobile, along with its production year and corresponding financial implications, he would possess a concrete objective to pursue, increasing his likelihood of successful attainment.

Decide your dreams. It is essential for you to ascertain your life's priorities and identify the factors that, in your assessment, would enhance the quality of your life. These can encompass material items or even psychological transformations, but it is imperative that you possess the ability to envision them. For instance, should you seek happiness, it is imperative to scrutinize those elements in your life that engender unhappiness, for eliminating these may ultimately lead to the attainment of your goal. If your objective is to accrue additional wealth, may I inquire how much would be required for financial concerns to become negligible? It is imperative to possess a distinctly defined notion of your requirements, enabling you to envision it holistically within the framework of your idealized life.

This is applicable to various aspects of your life. Visualize it in your imagination. Please shut your eyes and fully immerse yourself in the experience, for it is crucial to perceive it as something palpable rather than an elusive yearning. Vague desires don't happen. Tangible goals do.

Make your goals tangible. Observe them, make physical contact with them, experience their flavor, or engage in whatever action is necessary to concretely manifest the objective within your mind. Please engage in the act of closing your eyes and engaging your mind in visualizing the desired outcome. This process of visualization plays a crucial role in enabling you to incline towards making deliberate choices that have the potential to significantly impact the trajectory of your future, leading you towards acquiring what you perceive as necessary.

Individuals who exhibit such behavior demonstrate resilience in navigating challenging circumstances and effectively surmounting barriers that would otherwise impede their pursuit of personal aspirations. They do not allow those obstacles to hinder their pursuit of success. Alternatively, they adapt their thought process to account for the shifting circumstances.

Strategies For Enhancing Visualization Proficiency

The act of visualizing is the means by which you can bring into existence and actualize the desired outcomes in your life. Visualization does not present any anomalies, peculiarity, or novelty. This is an action that you consistently perform on a daily basis, persistently engaging in it up until the present moment. Imagination is a remarkable endowment that empowers us to harness this inherent ability to draw towards us the desired outcomes. Visualization is an integral component of the creative energy intrinsic to the universe, whereby its persistent and consistent application can engender a reciprocal manifestation in your reality. What an exquisite present that is!

Visualizing does not necessitate the need to place faith in any external or superior entities beyond one's own self. While it is not necessary for one to subscribe to spiritual or metaphysical beliefs, it is important to refrain from confining oneself solely within the confines of scientific and purely logical explanations.

The sole prerequisite entails possessing a disposition inclined towards augmenting one's knowledge and broadening one's perspective in life, through fostering a mindset that remains receptive enough to engender a constructive demeanor.

Step 1. Set your goal.

The essence of visualization would be compromised in the absence of initially establishing a goal. Prior to taking any action, it is imperative that you attain utmost clarity within yourself regarding your true desires, preferences, or aspirations that you aim to acquire or manifest. What type of residence are you interested in inhabiting? What type of business would you like to establish? What attributes or qualities are you seeking in a potential spouse? What are your true desires and aspirations?

Your objective has the potential to encompass any aspiration, provided it aligns with your heartfelt desires and resonates with your innermost sentiments. Experiencing a sense of satisfaction and contentment upon reflection is a definitive indication that the object of contemplation aligns with your innermost desires.

It can also encompass various aspects, ranging from one's dwelling, employment, beneficial transformations, interpersonal connections, enhanced well-being, affluence, aesthetic appeal, sound physical condition, and beyond.

It is imperative to grasp the fact that the magnitude of your desired outcome does not influence its visualization. Whether an individual desires a lavish million-dollar residence or a humble cup of coffee, procuring either is entirely achievable on an equal footing.

Step 2. Ask

Embrace the belief that through the act of asking, one can receive. Foster a strong internal resolve to regard the mind as an elaborate repository, wherein you peruse its contents with intention, stating, 'I aspire to emulate such qualities,' or 'I desire to attain this specific occupation,' and so forth. It is solely your responsibility to set yourself on the path toward your goals, and this commencement is initiated by the selection of the specific path you intend to pursue. The treasure drawing technique elucidated in the third chapter proves to be advantageous for this stage. One may opt to sketch, reproduce, or meticulously trim images of desired objects such as a pristine automobile, an exquisite dwelling, a soulmate, a substantial financial reward, or any other aspiration, and skillfully arrange them in a visually captivating collage that remains within view on a daily basis.

Step 3. Create mental pictures.

In addition to crafting a visual representation board depicting your desires, it is also advisable to cultivate mental imagery of those aspirations. Attempt to gently shut your eyes and conjure mental imagery of the objects or experiences that you desire. Nevertheless, do not merely envision those matters. It is also imperative to engage in the practice of envisioning oneself capable of attaining and enjoying those experiences. In this procedure, it is imperative to experience a sense of well-being. This sense of well-being is what triggers the communication that leads to its realization for you. This sensation of well-being facilitates the novel experience of living those moments in the present, as if actively engaging in them within the tangible realm.

An additional significant factor is to perceive the situation or object in the current tense, as though you are presently encountering it in the desired manner. You will come to appreciate that the sensation you are presently encountering mirrors precisely the emotion you will experience upon the actualization of those envisioned scenarios! Envision yourself immersed in the desired circumstances. Should you find yourself lying in your bed, it is possible to evoke a visualization wherein you perceive yourself situated upon an enchanting island in the Maldives, beholding the resplendent sight of the setting sun. Experience the emotions that will inevitably arise when the event occurs. Feel it NOW!

Please bear in mind that the human mind is incapable of discerning between genuine experiences and those generated purely through imagination. If one repeatedly engages in such actions, they are gradually establishing a connection with oneself, as the universe has aligned itself to facilitate their occurrence.

Step 4. Do it every day.

Doesn't it provide a sense of delight to mentally envisage the objects or experiences that you desire? Fortunately, performing this task on a daily basis remains imperative. Another crucial aspect to be acquainted with is the regularity of its execution. It is imperative to allocate a minimum of ten minutes each day to engage in visualizing one's desired objectives. For a duration of ten minutes, please shut your eyes and engage in the mental exercise of envisioning the life that you desire to lead. It is imperative not to overlook the crucial element: experiencing a sense of well-being.

What Does The Creative Visualization Technique Entail?

The concept of creative visualization pertains to the act or routine of deliberately shaping an individual's desires and thoughts in order to exert an influence on the external world. This technique serves as a fundamental and highly efficacious method underlying positive thinking, extensively adopted by contemporary athletes around the globe to enhance performance.

Allow us to engage in a comprehensive examination of the multifaceted components of Creative Visualization as it pertains to the contemporary fabric of our lives.

This refers to the practice of employing one's thoughts to envision precise occurrences or behaviors taking place in their life. Legal professionals recommend employing a comprehensive strategy to articulate one's aspirations or intentions, subsequently engaging in repetitive visualization utilizing all sensory perceptions. In games, a golfer may employ mental imagery to effectively train their muscle memory.

Visualization routines or methodologies are also prevalent manifestations of spiritual engagement. The practice of utilizing intricate visualizations is employed within the context of Buddhism to attain enlightenment. Moreover, the utilization of visualization is widespread in the field of sports psychology.

A frequently observed grievance among individuals who are inclined to engage in this technique of creative visualization is the difficulty in generating or perceiving a vivid and satisfactory image. When they close their eyes, they perceive either hues or simply an empty visual field. They encounter difficulties when attempting to visualize. This is the juncture at which the essential particulars come into play. To date, our attention has been primarily directed towards the visualization or observation aspect, as it consistently intertwines with enhancing athletes' performance. However, it is worth noting that creative visualization represents an equally potent technique for attaining any desired aspiration or objective. For example, you display a strong resolve towards securing alternative employment.

You have scheduled a designated time for visualization. You are expected to close your eyes and imagine yourself desiring to visualize an image of your new job, only to be met with disappointment. The greater your inclination towards "observing," the increasingly vacant your mental canvas becomes. It is crucial to bear in mind that each individual possesses five senses.

In the event that visual perception of the new job is unattainable, auditory comprehension thereof is an alternative. Consider a hypothetical scenario where you engage in an interpersonal dialogue with a colleague or a person holding a higher position within a professional setting. Visualize yourself engaged in a profound dialogue, articulately portraying your own essence to others with profound self-assurance and proficiency. The audience is exhibiting the expected favorable response that aligns with your conjectured ideal circumstances.

I must assert that the scent of the task you are attempting to envision is detectable. In fact, the envisioned conversation carries with it a certain fragrance, evoking the sensations of having a coffee apparatus nearby or walking to the pantry with a colleague.

Another approach to enhance your job satisfaction is by cultivating a positive mindset. For instance, envision yourself positioned next to your designated desk, confidently holding a large cup of tea or coffee, engaging in a successful conversation with your colleagues.

Now, as you engage with your visualization through tactile or auditory senses, I encourage you to perceive yourself effectively performing in the desired position or occupation, albeit exclusively visualizing a dominant hue of red. Prompt introspection regarding the symbolic connotations attributed to the color red. Does the matter pertain to my recent employment opportunity? Subsequently, you will come to the realization that the shirt being worn by your colleague, with whom you were engaged in conversation, is indeed the same one.

You were unaware, yet you observed it. Reality was revealed later. It is noticeable, observed, heard, and perceived through scent the nature of your new post or job. This aligns with your preferences.

I have been informed that it is imperative for us to engage in diligent and regular practice of Creative visualization, as this technique predominantly pertains to the concept of conducting mental rehearsals. Individuals employed in theatrical settings, such as directors, actors, and technical personnel, possess a profound appreciation for the intrinsic value of rehearsal. And, they rehearse often. They do not rely on chance when it comes to rehearsing.

They consistently establish a predetermined schedule and ensure its implementation. Initially, rehearsals are frequently scheduled. Individuals frequently fail to remember their dialogue; on occasion, actors do not thoroughly embody the personas they portray.

Through consistent and regular rehearsals or practice sessions, the quality of performances tends to enhance. In the end, as a result of their regularly scheduled and diligently practiced rehearsals, they gradually lose sight of the fact that they are actively engaged in a theatrical production and seamlessly immerse themselves in the art of the play.

It is a remarkable testament to the exceptional quality of the creative visualization when consistently and diligently applied during regular, predetermined intervals.

The researchers have documented the phenomenon of self-fulfilling prophecy, recognized as an inherent force within individuals. The fundamental tenet is to acknowledge that one's beliefs about oneself or certain circumstances, whether negative or positive, exert a significant influence on one's behavior, ultimately driving the transformation of those beliefs into reality.

For example, if a student harbors concerns about failing the exam, it is likely that their study habits would be adversely affected, resulting in a decrease in the amount of information they retain. Furthermore, the perspective that they would fail the experiment leads to an onset of anxiety, which consequently impairs brain functionality. The student's performance on the research is compromised significantly due to an inadequate amount of effort, making it highly probable that the student would fail the examination.

This theory appears to be most cogent when considering the strong correlation between the developmental stage of self-assurance and the corresponding convictions individuals hold about their own identities. If an individual lacks any confidence in their ability to pass the exam, it can be deduced that they lack trust or faith in themselves, which diminishes their engagement in behaviors that facilitate successful completion of the test, thereby reducing their efficacy. They may exhibit less frequent engagement in learning activities, fail to allocate the requisite amount of time for studying, or fail to capitalize on the advantages of collaborating with their study group.

However, the implementation of visualization techniques has the potential to transform an unproductive self-fulfilling prophecy into a constructive self-fulfilling prophecy. For example, on a regular basis and with a high level of attention to detail, effectively depicting an individual's persona is generating significant satisfaction in the evaluation process.

The level of self-confidence would be enhanced.

There is a perception among individuals that individuals with confident personalities prioritize their sense of capability rather than pursuing perfection wholeheartedly. In such an instance, they would successfully complete the test, although it may not necessarily equate to achieving the highest score within the class.

An exemplification of a highly effective approach for excelling in the examination is conducting a comprehensive study. We ought to organize the information into a document and ensure the folder's safekeeping within a designated compartment. If caught in a difficult situation during an examination, one can adopt a technique of closing the eyes, engaging in deep contemplation, or mentally picturing the folder stored in a drawer, only to retrieve it later with the necessary answer. This theory facilitates the development of novel neural pathways, whereby employing visualization can enhance problem-solving proficiency, resulting in accurate solutions.

What Changes?

In employing the technique of visualization, it is imperative to cultivate unwavering faith on a daily basis in respect to every single element depicted on your vision board. Even in the face of adversity, one must persevere with unwavering belief. There exists a highly justifiable rationale behind this. Once you begin to harbor disbelief or discard those convictions, your vibrational energy diminishes, prompting a regression to your previous behaviors.

What changes?

Let us endeavor to elucidate this matter through logical analysis. When an individual holds the conviction that they possess the ability to overcome any obstacle, they typically possess the capacity to do so. If one approaches an interview with the belief that they lack the necessary qualifications for the position, their prospects of securing the job become diminished. When one cultivates the perspective that they possess the utmost qualifications sought by the company for the position, a cognitive shift occurs that alters the intensity of their mental energies, ultimately enabling them to exude an aura of confidence and competence, thereby enhancing their prospects of securing the job. It is just as straightforward as that. The alteration that has been effected pertains to the core essence of your being. You assume the identity of an individual who emerges victorious, secures employment, or experiences inner contentment.

Things to avoid

It is not within the realm of possibility for an individual to assert an identity that is fundamentally incongruous with their physical capabilities. For instance, if one is vertically challenged, there will be no further increase in stature. Nonetheless, directing your attention towards other aspects of your existence results in the enhancement of your stature rather than your physical attributes. If you desire to have curly hair despite being naturally straight-haired, you can indeed achieve it through the process of perming, which is considered acceptable and effective for attaining the desired curls. However, it is vital to acknowledge that maintaining and caring for permed hair requires ongoing effort and attention. What you possess innately is immutable.

Nevertheless, it is within your capacity to alter the perception others hold of you by fostering a steadfast belief in your affirmations. I recall witnessing a woman of notably diminutive stature. She possessed ambitious aspirations, which she successfully actualized, establishing herself as an accomplished individual of remarkable stature. Her magnificence was unrelated to her stature. Therefore, you have the ability to embody all of your aspirations, while refraining from entertaining beliefs that contradict the laws of physics. It is highly improbable for any changes in your height to occur overnight. Nevertheless, should one desire to achieve a commanding presence and garner attention, the following options may prove viable.

Never cease believing in the power of your affirmation. The aforementioned statements are expressed using the current tense. These are not wishes. These are beliefs. When one ceases to believe, their energy diminishes significantly and there may arise the need to commence anew. Hence, it is imperative that you possess unwavering conviction in your declarations. Strive to maintain independence from external influences and remain resilient in the face of discouragement. Embrace the freedom to manifest your desired identity, and consequently, you shall attain all that you aspire to possess. When one permits external influences to permeate their dreams, the authenticity of those dreams diminishes and subsequently, their dedication and fervor in pursuing them also wanes.

The enumerated process comprises the subsequent actions necessary to fulfill all of your desires:

Engage in a comprehensive depiction of your desired outcome. Observe it, extend your hand and make contact with it. It is of paramount importance to fully engage oneself in envisioning and embracing the desired future lifestyle. Enterprises formulate vision statements with a specific objective in mind. It is an action taken to ensure that all individuals are aligned and working towards the same goals. In order to manifest one's distinctive visions, it is imperative to possess lucidity and a comprehensive understanding of every intricate aspect of said vision, enabling one to actualize it.

Have unwavering faith in your vision, channeling all your fervor. This zeal enables its transformation into tangible form. The force of passion propels individuals towards their desired aspirations in life, and it is imperative that one approaches their daily perusal of the vision board with unabashed fervor.

Pursue it with utmost determination and commitment. When your mental disposition is appropriately aligned, this will not pose as a challenging endeavor. You will wholeheartedly dedicate yourself to the envisioned image and effectively convince others of your unwavering passion and determination.

It is not as frivolous as it may initially appear. Individuals have the ability to manifest a wide array of visualizations, albeit by employing unwavering ardor and conviction. One must not relinquish that belief, even when faced with adversity in life. Individuals who possess a fervent ardor do not allow the obstacles of existence to impede their progress, as they are cognizant that their aspirations transcend these minor setbacks. They possess a formidable resilience beyond the described situation. Primarily, everything undergoes transformation. The perspective from which you perceive life and the perspective from which life perceives you undergoes changes, signifying the convergence of all the elements in your life. You have transitioned from being perceived as an idealist to an individual known for taking action. Your positive demeanor resonates with everyone, and your determined attitude is apparent to both the bank manager whom you successfully convince to fund your idea, and to all those who offer their unwavering support on your journey towards achieving your unique form of success. I currently have a greater number of acquaintances and companions in my existence than I have previously experienced, owing to my unwavering faith in my abilities and the aspiration I had conceived many years ago, which retains its vitality as greatly as it did on the very inception of my ambitions.

Establish Your Narrative

Having comprehended the significance of identifying the intended recipients of your design, the subsequent essential task is to ascertain the precise message or objective you aim to convey to your target audience. It is imperative to possess a clear understanding of your central concept or storyline prior to commencing the design process. Having this knowledge will enable you to determine the most effective approach for conveying ample information to the audience through your design. Furthermore, having a clear understanding of what you intend to communicate will provide you with insight into the appropriate manner in which to craft its presentation. As an illustration, would you like to accentuate a juxtaposition or pattern, an evolution over a period, or perhaps an association? You will ascertain this once you have determined your message or main concept.

Now that you have clarified the key individuals and elements involved in your visual representation, let us progress towards examining the methodology. How can one effectively construct a data narrative that includes relevant context? A strong narrative centers around the art of captivating storytelling. A plethora of outstanding designs adhere to a traditional progression comprising of three fundamental stages: initial presentation, core message delivery, and ultimate summation.

1. Introduction/Background: Within this segment of your data narrative, the objective is to establish a solid groundwork for the insights and facts that you intend to present to your audience. This segment facilitates the establishment of the necessary

foundation for the comprehension and perception of your visualization by the observer.

2. The pivotal occurrence or the illuminating moment: The revelation point is the focal event of the data visualization. In order for the design or visualization to be remarkable, it should evoke a sense of awe or facilitate a moment of comprehension within the viewers. This can solely be accomplished if the visualization incorporates novel and heretofore undisclosed informational aspects.

3. Final remarks/Invocation: It is imperative to attain a sense of resolution in concluding your data narrative, akin to a impactful conclusion of an oration. If one were to design a visual element with the intention of evoking emotional responses from the audience, it is imperative that the concluding part of the presentation succeeds in stirring excitement among individuals and effectively impels them to take action based on their emotional state. Could

they consider visiting a website, endorsing a petition, endeavoring to bring about change, making a strategic business decision, or contributing to a cause through a donation? The visual should effectively impart to the viewers the understanding of how to utilize the concise piece of information that has been presented to them, as conveyed by you, the designer.

After obtaining a preliminary outline of your intended message and the essential outcomes you desire your audience to glean from your visual representation, amalgamate this framework with the graph format that best communicates your concepts in the utmost efficient manner.

Selecting Appropriate Data For Effective Visualization: A Guide

In drawing an analogy between your data visualization and a museum exhibition, your data can be likened to the entirety of the collection, encompassing even the parts that were not showcased. All the prospective artistic pieces have been amassed, organized, and meticulously selected or rejected for inclusion in an exhibition. In the event that there is an insufficient amount of data presented in a visual context, it becomes considerably arduous for the observer to construct a precise depiction of the narrative being conveyed by the data. It does not imply that you consolidate all your data into a single visual representation, rendering it once again incomprehensible. Rather, acquire the skill of selecting the most pertinent information from your dataset.

Carefully select and curate your dataset, considering what is suitable for your 'exhibition.' At times, it may be necessary to manually incorporate additional data in order to ensure that you do not overlook any interesting variables that could enhance visualization.

In the book Data Sketches, Nadieh Bremer presents a comprehensive visualization illustrating each of her travel experiences from birth until present. As the information retrieved pertained to personal data, she had to gather every piece of it by hand, which presented an occasion to create an engaging and compelling experience. The evident data points to be utilized include dates, destinations, and duration of the journeys. However, Nadieh incorporated   supplementary information such as her travel companions, the objectives of the trips, and the level of her satisfaction. By adopting this approach, you can enhance the visualization of your data narrative and broaden the scope for establishing emotional connections with your audience. Acquire the skill of effectively analyzing your data, removing unnecessary elements, and incorporating the data that best aligns with your conceptualization and visualization. Assume the role of the curator for your own exhibition.

To ascertain the accuracy of the data, it is imperative to first gain a comprehensive understanding of the various classifications of data and their interconnections. Within the realm of data, various classifications exist. However, when it comes to creating data visualizations, it is essential to bear in mind the two fundamental classifications: quantitative and qualitative. Quantitative data pertains to values that are quantifiable or computable in numerical terms. Conversely, qualitative data pertains to data that is classified based on groupings, categories, or types.

Once you have determined the nature of the data you are dealing with, it becomes essential to establish a linkage between your dataset. Does the data exhibit any discernible patterns or indicative of a developing relationship? There are various methods to tackle this issue.

Non-sequential - a categorization lacking discernible arrangement

Ranking - a sequential arrangement of multiple groups according to their relative importance or significance.

Correlation refers to the presence of a positive, negative, or null association between two or more variables.

Deviation - elucidating the interrelationship of the data with a particular focus on the disparity from the average

Distribution refers to the manner in which the data is dispersed around a central value.

Temporal data series - a sequential arrangement of data points tied to chronological order, often utilized for predictive analysis

Utilize this correlation to aid in determining the suitable usage of charts or graphs, and to discern instances where textual explanations are more pertinent. Furthermore, implementing a well-devised approach that reduces visual overload while maximizing the transmission of meaningful content can be achieved by utilizing a harmonious combination of visual elements and written text. This equilibrium ensures that your visualization remains lucid and interconnected.

Likewise, an excessive amount of information or data condensed within a confined area overwhelms the viewer with an excess of visual clutter. It elicits a similar outcome as attempting to perceive your acquaintance amidst a crowd of concertgoers. It is evident that they are attempting to communicate with you, yet the cacophony generated by the surrounding multitude and the amplification system overwhelms the intended message. Utilize the fundamental concepts of design and arrangement in order to align the elements of your chart or graph in a manner that facilitates seamless navigation and comprehension for the viewer. A strategy worth exploring is to commence with a gray or monotone aesthetic. Prioritize maintaining an overarching perspective on placement and flow initially, subsequently enhancing through the deliberate utilization of colors, patterns, and complementary elements. Direct your attention towards the fundamental aspects, or the core elements, of your visualization, and afterwards incorporate visual elements to prompt a deliberate and attentive examination of all the components comprising your data visualization.

The Application Of Visualization Techniques In Achieving Success

You have acquired valuable strategies to enhance your creativity and employ meditation techniques effectively. However, you are likely eager to explore concrete methodologies to engage in creative visualization, thereby striving towards the achievement of your imminent success. Now, we shall proceed with elucidating a straightforward approach to seamlessly integrate all of these elements and achieve remarkable results for you.

Visualize

After achieving the appropriate mental disposition, commence your visualizations. Ensure that you visualize yourself in the desired situation with utmost precision and specificity. Envision, with utmost detail, every aspect ranging from the visual elements to the olfactory sensations, and consider thoroughly every facet of your perception and the myriad of possibilities in which your vision will transpire flawlessly. Avoid fixating on any negative aspects; redirect your attention towards wholeheartedly embracing the positive outcome that is bound to occur. The key to achieving success lies in cultivating robust and constructive energy, which necessitates diligent efforts to sustain such sentiments and shield oneself from any encroaching negativity.

Relax and Prepare

Ensure that you are in the appropriate mental state when you initially commence the process of envisioning the desired course of events. Establish an ambiance that cultivates serenity and instills a sense of positivity. Prepare and arrange your designated meditation space to your liking, ensuring optimal comfort. It is advisable to engage in meditation for a minimum duration of 5-10 minutes, or potentially extend the practice if so desired. It is imperative to ensure that one maintains a state of concentration, calmness, and optimism.

Visualize During the Day

It is imperative to consider your goals not only during the active engagement in a creative visualization session, but also on other occasions. It is advisable to envision oneself attaining success while engaging in everyday tasks, ensuring a steadfast belief in the attainability of these aspirations. Through the cultivation of self-assurance and the anticipation of favorable outcomes, eventual attainment of these positive events is ensured. Once more, it should be understood that not all desired outcomes can be achieved instantaneously. Nonetheless, an accelerated manifestation may be realized by wholeheartedly embracing the conviction that they will be realized.

It is crucial to bear in mind that you have the ability to actively bring about positive transformations in your life. A recent study conducted with multiple cohorts of athletes revealed that the group integrating their routine training regimen with an equal amount of time dedicated to visualization demonstrated superior performance compared to groups that allocated little to no time for visualization. These findings are expected to provide you with the assurance that your objectives can indeed be achieved through the implementation of these identical strategies. When engaging in self-reflective exercises amidst the course of your day to reinforce your objectives, several supplementary factors can provide assistance as well.

Make a Board

If you encounter an image or text that evokes a powerful association with the objectives you are earnestly pursuing, it is advisable to preserve it. Create a tangible vision board that compiles all of these elements to enhance your ability to channel your energy effectively.

Having a clear vision of your objectives can serve as a motivating factor to exert greater effort in attaining them. This affords you a comprehensive visual representation to concentrate on, further intensifying the sentiment that your dreams are readily attainable. In undertaking this action, you are also affording yourself a continuous prompt to maintain a positive outlook and to maintain receptiveness towards new prospects that could otherwise elude your attention.

Tell it to Yourself

Regularly prioritize thoughts of your achievement and success. During your morning shower, allocate your time to indulging in reveries centered around them. When preparing oneself in front of the mirror, articulate the words audibly. When you find yourself inside the vehicle, please reiterate those words audibly. Incorporate these visualizations into your daily routine consistently.

Write EVERYTHING Down

The written word holds great influence over a significant number of individuals. Please document precisely the objectives you wish to achieve and review them periodically if you perceive any deviation. Continue to further develop your thoughts in your journal and derive pleasure from your meticulous explorations. Additionally, this can enhance your dedicated periods of creative visualizations by providing you with increased concentration for contemplation.

Utilizing Creative Visualization As A Strategy For Achieving Victory

You have acquired valuable strategies for enhancing your imagination and are now equipped with simple yet effective methodologies to cultivate your meditation proficiency. However, you are likely eager to acquire concrete techniques that harness the power of creative visualization for the purpose of attaining the success that awaits you. Allow us to present an uncomplicated approach to integrating all of these elements and realize their remarkable potential for you.

Relax and Prepare

Ensure that you are in a suitable mental state upon initially commencing the process of envisioning the desired course of events. Establish a conducive setting that cultivates a sense of calmness and instills a state of positivity. Establish a designated space for your meditation practice and ensure utmost comfort within it. Strive to engage in a meditation practice for a minimum duration of 5 to 10 minutes, or extend the session further according to your personal preference. It is imperative to ensure that you maintain a state of attentiveness, calmness, and optimism.

Visualize

Once you have achieved the appropriate mental state, commence your visualizations. Ensure that you envision yourself residing within the desired situation with utmost precision. Envision vividly the entirety of sensory impressions, encompassing the visual imagery, olfactory perceptions, and emotional responses that shall be encountered upon its occurrence. Devote ample time to fully apprehend each component of your vision, along with every conceivable favorable outcome it can entail. Do not dwell on any negative aspects; rather, ensure your unwavering commitment towards the imminent positive outcome. The key to achieving success lies in cultivating a resilient, optimistic mindset, wherein one diligently pursues positive emotions while steadfastly guarding against the infiltration of negativity.

Don't Stop

Creative visualization is not a sporadic practice effective in yielding results. Endeavor to incorporate it into your daily regimen. It is imperative to maintain a continual flow of positive thoughts, a state that can only be achieved by constant immersion in them. Persist even if the duration seems prolonged beyond your initial expectations; persevere and maintain the focus on visualizing your objectives.

Visualize During the Day

It is imperative to contemplate your objectives not only during active engagement in a creative visualization session, but also during various other junctures. One ought to visualize oneself achieving success while performing everyday tasks and maintain a steadfast belief in the attainability of these aspirations. By harboring such self-assurance and nurturing a positive outlook on life, one can ultimately manifest desirable outcomes. Once more, it should be noted that the realization of all your desired outcomes may not transpire promptly, but by fully immersing yourself in the conviction that they will occur, you can expedite their manifestation.

MEDITATION FOR THE DISPOSAL OF NEGATIVE THOUGHTS

Attention to the presenter: Kindly observe a pause of 15 seconds between each sentence, unless instructed otherwise. The portion highlighted in yellow ought to be enunciated at a deliberate pace, affording the recipient an ample opportunity to comprehend and commit the sentences to memory.

This particular meditation has been carefully devised to facilitate the elimination of any lingering negative emotions and thoughts that may have inadvertently eluded resolution in previous meditation sessions.

I kindly request that you locate a suitable location characterized by comfort and tranquility, in which you may take repose for the duration of the following half-hour.

Assume a seated or supine position on the floor, ensuring that your entire body is firmly in contact with the surface.

Please allow your muscles to unwind, calmly elongate and relieve tension in your fingers and arms, followed by your feet and legs, your shoulders and torso, and ultimately your head and neck. (To be enunciated with measured pace and deliberate pauses after each anatomical reference)

Relieve any residual tension by drawing in a deep breath and subsequently exhaling, allowing yourself to fully relax.

If it is possible, please shut your eyes. In the event that you prefer to refrain from closing your eyes, it is possible to direct your attention towards an object situated immediately in your vicinity. Ensure that you maintain focus on the designated object for the entire duration of the meditation session.

In the event that you perceive a lack of concentration during the exercise, redirect your attention to your breathing rhythm and regain mastery over your thoughts.

Now, I kindly request that you clear your mind by engaging in the practice of visualizing and observing the thoughts traversing your consciousness.

Examine each of them individually, recognize their presence, and then release them.

If you perceive that your cognitive faculties hinder the release of your thoughts, you can grant yourself authorization to segregate them into a distinct compartment, to be addressed following the conclusion of this meditative session.

Once you have achieved a state of tranquility and mental clarity, redirect your attention and concentrate on your breathing: Inhale naturally and at your regular pace; retain your breath for a count of four seconds (1...2...3...4) and subsequently release it gradually through your mouth.

And once again, perform inhalation, maintaining it for a duration of four counts, and subsequently exhale gradually via your oral cavity.

Once more: take in breath at your regular tempo, maintain for four counts, and release gradually. (Reiterate for a duration of one minute, with intervals of 15 seconds.)

Continue to practice this breathing technique until it becomes ingrained, resulting in a serene and tranquil state of mind and body.

Once you perceive a sense of unhindered respiratory motion, divert your focus inwardly. Conduct a concise self-assessment to ascertain the current state of your inner being, and allocate a few moments to discern whether any impediments in the flow of your bodily energy remain unresolved from yesterday's meditation.

All of these inhibitions stem from prior agonies and suffering, their deep-rooted existence impacting the course of your life. It is imperative to address these matters in order to foster a constructive mindset and cultivate a self-assured perspective on your forthcoming endeavors.

Now endeavor to sensitively perceive these obstructed areas, individually and sequentially, discerning their specific location and the associated memories they evoke.

Do you experience both emotional and physical discomfort in these regions of your body? Do you perceive the blocks to be uniformly localized, or are they dispersed across different regions within your body?

In order to initiate the restoration of your emotional liberty, I kindly request that you select the most significant point of distress and energetic impediment within your physical being.

Place your hands upon the designated area, allowing yourself to inhale and exhale at a leisurely and serene pace. (Allow a 20-second interval for contemplation.)

While maintaining your hands in that position, I kindly request that you allow your heart to be receptive to the positive energy that we cultivated throughout the previous sessions of meditation.

If you can, you can also use your secret chosen word to make this process a faster one.

Enunciate the word internally with deliberate deliberation on three occasions, whilst acknowledging the ensuing emotions surging within your heart.

Experience the sensation of your heart becoming imbued with a positive energy that serves as a reminder of the multitude of things you possess for which to express gratitude in your life, as well as an acknowledgement of the various positive qualities that define your character.

Allow that identical fervor to emanate from within the depths of your heart and extend its reach towards those barriers and regions plagued by anguish.

Guide the momentum using the gentle contact of your hands, positioning them at the locations where you perceive the strongest need for therapeutic intervention.

Direct your attention towards that specific area: How do you perceive the sensations that arise when the energy intersects with the discomfort and barriers? Is there any recollection emerging within your thoughts? Can you perceive any visual representations or recollections?

Please be assured that in this present moment, you can feel secure and shielded, as long as you exercise your will and readiness to prevent any adverse occurrences.

Our aim is to facilitate the release of emotional and physical burdens that are impeding your progress and connection to a past that holds no relevance to your present circumstances.

Now, allocate a brief period of time to observe the visual representations and cognitive patterns that are manifesting within your consciousness as the regions of obstruction are liberated. (A brief intermission of half a minute.)

Abstain from censoring or passing judgment upon your observations and emotions; channel your positivity and embrace any thoughts that enter your mind instead.

Allow yourself to experience any emotional or physical anguish. They no longer possess the capacity to cause harm; you are now prepared to emancipate yourself from their grasp.

If necessary, please do not hesitate to articulate your emotions using any appropriate means available to you; you may now release these thoughts through tears, cries, or even physical gestures.

You have attained the readiness to liberate yourself from these thoughts and ideas.

Observe the congregation of thoughts within your mind, then select the one that you wish to liberate initially.

Observe the sentiment presented; visualize the imagery it evokes and silently recite this phrase thrice in your mind:

I hereby choose to eradicate this thought from my existence, relinquishing any and all feelings of guilt, fear, anger, or any adverse emotions attached to this recollection in my mental and physical being." (Recite thrice, with 15-second intervals.)

Upon completion, you may proceed to recite the aforementioned sentence audibly or silently, for a total of three repetitions.

"I have relinquished all the judgments, attachments and impediments that I have personally cultivated, accumulated and embraced in relation to this recollection." (Recite thrice.)

Take a few moments to relinquish any remaining energy and proceed to choose another recollection or idea to address and liberate yourself from, when you deem it appropriate.

Envision that concept vividly within your thoughts; perceive both the emotional and physical manifestations, subsequently center your focus and silently recite the phrase internally thrice:

"I hereby relinquish this thought from my existence, and detach myself from all feelings of remorse, trepidation, resentment, or any variant adversarial sentiment tied to this recollection within my psyche and physical being." (Recite thrice, with 15-second pauses between repetitions.)

Once you have concluded, you may proceed to reiterate the aforementioned phrase audibly or internally, thrice more.

"I have now liberated my mind and body from all the judgments, attachments, and hindrances I have constructed, gathered, and embraced concerning this recollection." (Repeat three times at 15 second intervals.)

Engage in this process with every single memory and thought that is currently occupying your mind, until none remain. Allow for a brief moment of silence.

Please ensure that you incorporate this sentence at the onset of the procedure: "

I hereby affirm my intention to relinquish any lingering negativity, be it guilt, fear, anger, or any other adverse emotion tied to this recollection, and release it from my mental and physical being.

And subsequently, after completing the aforementioned task:

I am currently liberated in both my mental and physical state, as I have successfully relinquished all the judgments, attachments, and constraints that I have personally formed, accumulated, and acknowledged with regard to this particular recollection." (Pause for one minute.)

Ensure that the unrestricted flow of positive energy emanating from your innermost being is unencumbered at present, and that any obstacles and residual pain from the past have been eradicated from both your mental and physical being, in order to be adequately prepared to commence constructing a fresh and promising future during tomorrow's session.

Please allocate a brief period of time to conduct a prompt self-review, and once completed, take a moment to rest, allowing both your mind and body to settle. Please allow for a brief interval of 30 seconds.

Direct your attention back to your breath: take in a breath at your regular rhythm, then pause for a duration of 4 seconds (1...2...3...4), and subsequently release the breath gradually through your mouth.

And reiterate: take a deep breath in, retain it for a count of four, and subsequently release it gently through your mouth.

Reiterate the instructions: Inhale at your customary rhythm, retain the breath for a duration of four seconds, and proceed to exhale gradually. (Reiterate the task at 15-second intervals for a duration of one minute.)

Grant yourself the authorization to reestablish a connection with the present moment, commencing with your physical self: perceive the sensation of gravity grounding you; swiftly assess your current state of being.

Reclaim cognizance of your surroundings, encompassing all olfactory and auditory stimuli.

Allow yourself a brief interlude to relish the process of returning, and when you feel prepared, either open your eyes or redirect your attention from the object to your own being.

Inhale deeply and expel any residual tension as you exhale.

You may now rise to your feet and firmly press your soles against the floor to reestablish a sense of grounding.

Congratulations on successfully concluding the third segment of this remarkable expedition!

Allow me to extend a warm welcome to the fourth day of this transformative expedition centered around cultivating optimistic thoughts and attaining emotional liberation.

The purpose of today's exercise is to equip you for upcoming challenges and to manifest your optimistic vision of the future.

Prior to commencing, I kindly request that you cleanse your personal energy of any residual impacts from yesterday's meditation, and ready yourself for today's session by engaging in our customary introductory exercise:

How To Harness The Power Of The Law Of Attraction Through The Practice Of Visualization

An approach to implementing the law of attraction in your life is to practice the technique of envisioning your aspirations. This topic was deliberated upon in the film titled "The Secret"; however, the method of visualizing was not explicitly referenced. Below, we present seven sequential measures to facilitate the process of visualizing, enabling you to effectively employ the principles of the law of attraction.

Firstly, establish the desired visualization.

Whenever you embark on visualization, it is imperative to have a clearly defined objective or objectives that you aspire to manifest. For instance, consider this scenario: while on your midday break, you may wish to envision two scenarios. Firstly, indulging in a delightful evening with your loved ones later today, and secondly, accomplishing exceptional work on the ongoing project you are currently engaged in.

Step 2 - Locate a serene location.

Locate a serene environment where you can experience minimal disruptions or interruptions from others. Frequently, I opt for locations such as the bed, prior to and upon awakening, or my personal study space within my residence where I am assured of an uninterrupted environment.

Step 3 - Engage in Mental Relaxation Techniques

Prior to engaging in visualization, it is essential to cleanse your mind of any distractions that may hinder the process. If you are experiencing concerns regarding a report or a meeting, it is advisable to calmly take a seat, unwind, and redirect your focus away from these distractions.

Step 4 - Please close your eyes and commence visualizing

Kindly, gently close your eyes to induce a state of utmost relaxation, and begin to contemplate your aspirations. Envision the manner in which you conduct yourself upon achieving the ultimate outcome of your aspiration. If one is contemplating the acquisition of an automobile, it would be prudent to consider the act of operating said vehicle and the various destinations to be frequented.

Proceed to the fifth step - Engage in the Visualization

The utmost significance lies in actively experiencing the visualization. Observe the manner in which you are responding while manifesting your aspirations. Observe the level of joy you experience while operating your recently acquired vehicle. The sensation of gripping the steering wheel, the fragrance of the gasoline, the auditory output emanating from the CD system. These emotions are the source of the positive energy you emit to the universe.

Step 6 - Observe with vigilance.

Subsequently, emerge from the state of visualization. If your contemplation has been accurate, you will experience a sense of authenticity in what transpired.

This is the sensation one desires. Each time you engage in visualization, strive to evoke this sensation upon culmination.

Step 7 - Continue

While engaged in professional or domestic activities, it is advisable to maintain an attitude of living out one's aspirations. Behave as if you are presently in possession of the new car, have already been promoted, and are presently engaged in a vacation with your family.

Step 8 - Ensure precise clarity regarding the precise objectives you seek to achieve.

Setting a clearly defined goal is essential in the process of Visualization. It can encompass a range of pursuits, such as wealth accumulation or the quest for a compatible life partner. Ensure that you record it clearly on a piece of paper or construct a visual representation, such as a vision board, in order to establish and visualize your objective with precision. If it pertains to financial earnings, what is the specific amount you desire to acquire? If it is eliciting the attention of your compatible partner, what is their physical appearance, habitual patterns, personality traits, and behavioral tendencies? It would be advisable to document your objective and strive to provide explicit details while maintaining a subjective perspective as much as possible.

By adhering to these outlined procedures, one has indeed attained proficiency in the technique of visualization and acquired the ability to effectively employ the law of attraction through visualization.

Journaling & Visualization

To achieve the realization of your desired life, it is simply a matter of acquiring this writing instrument and acquiring the knowledge and technique necessary to induce self-hypnosis, thereby drawing in the desired outcomes. This phenomenon is commonly referred to as attraction scripting, a technique employed to accelerate the manifestation of one's desired outcomes beyond previously perceived capabilities. Visual writing or journaling involves actively stimulating and engaging your nervous system through the senses. So, it effectively prompts the activation of your conscious mind, enabling access to the subconscious realm and facilitating the modification of predetermined patterns within your subconscious mind, thereby fostering transformative changes in your life.

I would employ this scripting methodology in my personal affairs and various other endeavors. In a straightforward manner, my practice entails retrieving a journal and inscribing at the header, "I express immense gratitude for the state my life has achieved." Furthermore, I shall endeavor to play pleasant and melodious music as I undertake the task at hand. Discover music that resonates with your personal preferences as a means to unwind and initiate the process. Subsequently, proceed to exclusively articulate your aspirations for your future existence using exclusively the future tense.

Please dedicate approximately 20 to 30 minutes to this task, as it may require three to five minutes for you to familiarize yourself with the initial steps and a few days for you to fully acclimate to the concept. The time required for achieving your desires may be prolonged due to the influence of your conscious mind and the ingrained patterns that shape your perception of the world. Your conscious mind may raise doubts by reminding you that you have not attained these desires yet. To counter this, it is advisable to mentally immerse yourself in a state of gratitude, specifically focusing on vividly envisioning the details of your ideal romantic relationship, financial success, career progression, dream home, preferred location, or the type of car you desire. Delve deeply into intricate specifics, and continue to expound upon them. Please feel free to reiterate your thoughts, employing any necessary measures to alleviate any preoccupations.

During my time in high school, I recall participating in an English class activity that stood out to me as the sole activity that I genuinely enjoyed. This particular activity pertained to what our instructor referred to as "creative writing." The educator would establish a predetermined time limit of 25 minutes and actively lead us in the process of writing. Previously, she would instruct me to freely write for a duration of 25 minutes, during which I would fabricate tales of the utmost peculiarity. However, such thoughts would never occur to me, and moreover, it was strictly prohibited to remove the pen from the paper.

You were required to continue writing, therefore I propose that you engage in practicing the very same activity. Please refrain from removing your pen from the paper. I am profoundly appreciative of the numerous blessings that have enriched my life, thus far. Moving forward, I shall proceed with writing, beginning with an expression of gratitude for all that I have experienced. Engage in conversation about any topic of your choosing while enjoying the serene ambiance of the picturesque sandy shore. Regardless of what it may be, immerse yourself in the task and dedicate 10 to 20 minutes to its completion. Every single solitary day. Engage in this daily routine and observe how, in a parallel manner to how you train your body to become more robust, you are training your mind to adapt to a new paradigm.

What is the mechanism by which a young child becomes cognizant of their given name, and what is the cognitive process through which a dog becomes aware of and responds to their designated name? The child's name is preserved by the parents of the guardians. The process of repetition leads to the assimilation of the information within the subconscious mind.

Reiterating concepts leads to the implantation of ideas into the subconscious mind, as they become indelibly imprinted upon it, and whatever aspects are imprinted upon your subconscious will manifest in your life. Similarly, the child's acquaintance with his name stems solely from consistent repetition. Consider a scenario in which the parents consistently refrain from addressing their child by their given name, explicitly stating that the child is to recall this particular instance as their sole introduction to their name, despite the child being a mere two years of age. Do you believe he will recollect his own name?

No, it signifies a recurring pattern where he starts to associate himself with the persona known as Joy. This represents my true identity. Consider another instance, what is your identity? Your thought. It is merely that you have associated yourself with a particular narrative in a similar fashion as Joy associated himself with his given name. Throughout the narrative, it is plausible that you have discerned a self-perception of being unlovable or experiencing considerable challenges in establishing and maintaining relationships. As a result of perceiving relationships as challenging, you have developed an unconscious inclination to distance yourself from them. You may have come to the determination that financial resources are scarce. One might possess a perception of oneself as unattractive, obese, aged, juvenile, or encounter challenges in the realm of acquiring knowledge. I regret to inform you that your likelihood of achieving success in this matter is significantly diminished.

It is conceivable that you possess a narrative with which you strongly associate, and over time, through recurrent recitation, akin to how a child repeatedly utters its name, a similar effect is achieved. The recurring invocation of that narrative upon which you have now associated yourself, has resulted in its assimilation as your prevailing state of existence.

The singular method by which change can be accomplished is to genuinely align oneself with the newly constructed narrative. Now, one can achieve this either by employing hypnotic writing techniques or by utilizing the Law of Attraction script. Commence with the initial sentence and derive enjoyment from it. Indulge in the moment and refrain from sharing; simply claim this as your own. The subsequent phase entails allowing it to be assimilated into your consciousness. Commence establishing a connection with the image. When you get connected to the picture in your mind over a long period of time, it will implant in the subconscious mind.

You are configuring it in a similar manner as one would configure a thermostat to maintain a temperature of 75 degrees. What functions does that thermostat perform? It will effectively maintain a temperature of 75 degrees within the room, regardless of the incoming air's temperature of 90 degrees, thus effectively combating warmth. The thermostat will activate and distribute chilled air to counteract the 90-degree temperature and maintain it at a comfortable level of 75 degrees. It is designed to maintain homeostasis. In a similar vein, when one possesses the ability to program one's life, it follows that the subconscious mind will exhibit a parallel pattern. It will ensure it behaves in accordance with your desires. Individuals who effortlessly manifest their desires possess an innate inclination ingrained within their subconscious.

Experience it - It is imperative to personally experience the intensity of your desire in order to truly achieve its full fruition. How is it possible to perceive or experience it? One can initiate the process by vividly envisioning the colors, sensations, textures, and joy, to the extent that their perception becomes palpable. Kindly perceive it in the present moment. Immerse yourself in the sensation of reliving that specific moment. This sensation will instill a sense of optimism within your subconscious, spurring expeditious manifestation.

Continuously envision - Is there any further need for me to stress it? It is essential that you engage in daily repetition. Should you find yourself engaged in matters of significance, there may be occasions where you inadvertently overlook it. However, it is necessary to perform this action on a daily basis. Continue your efforts until you have successfully accomplished your objective. The realization of this objective may require some time, yet it is incumbent upon you to wholeheartedly engage with this goal within the realm of your imagination.

Embrace the conviction that your desired outcome is within reach - By engaging in vivid mental imagery, you signal a genuine requirement for its manifestation in the physical realm. In order to attain this objective, it is imperative that you cultivate the belief that it is already within your possession. Envision a scenario in which you are already the proud owner of that automobile, or have already secured that desired position.

What impact does it have on your ability to form mental images? It evokes imagery within your subconscious mind, fostering a sense of personal ownership. Bear in mind that your subconscious mind is unable to discern between actuality and fantasy. Hence, your mind will give rise to a succession of positive emotions.

You will be presented with precise situations in which you can effectively bring about the manifestation of that objective. Having faith is of utmost significance when it comes to visualization, as it establishes the proper trajectory for your journey.